TO:

FROM:

DATE:

Coloring FAITH

PEACE
BE WITH YOU

An Inspirational COLORING BOOK
for STRESS RELIEF *and* CREATIVITY

ZONDERVAN®

ZONDERVAN

Peace Be with You
Copyright © 2021 by Zondervan

Requests for information should be addressed to:
Zondervan, *3900 Sparks Dr. SE, Grand Rapids, Michigan 49546*

ISBN 978-0-310-46034-3

Art direction and cover design: Jennifer Greenwalt

Interior illustrations: Suzanne Khushi, Lizzie Preston, Julianne St. Clair

Interior design: Phoebe Wetherbee

Printed in Canada
21 22 23 24 25 TC 10 9 8 7 6 5 4 3 2 1

INTRODUCTION

"Peace I leave with you; my peace I give you. I do not give to you as the world gives. Do not let your hearts be troubled and do not be afraid."

JOHN 14:27

We talk about finding peace all the time, especially these days, when modern life can be physically and emotionally exhausting. While there's nothing wrong with being busy or being plugged in to technology, the inundation of input can present challenges and often generates stress.

Stress affects our well-being and our health, so it's important to make time for self-care, to quiet our minds, connect with God, and spend time with His Word. Self-care not only revives our bodies, but it also gives us the space to truly unite our minds and spirits with God.

Because our brains often jump from topic to topic, task to task, many of us find it difficult to actually slow down and focus on one thing, let alone have time for deep thinking. That's why we've created this gorgeous coloring book—to quiet your mind and allow your spirit to breathe. Did you know that coloring has the ability to relax your brain? Coloring prompts a relaxed state similar to meditation and reduces anxious thoughts.

In these beautifully illustrated pages, you can reflect on peaceful images, on the movement of your own hands as you create stunning art, on God's unchanging Word, and on inspiring quotes that will encourage and uplift. We hope you'll read the words and feel motivated to pray or meditate on them while you color. More than anything, we hope this book will offer you calm moments that will form a closer connection with God while you create something beautiful.

Work through the pages in order from start to finish, or choose an image that speaks to you. Decorate your space with the colored pages, or give them as gifts to someone you love to share words of peace and beauty.

Want to share your artwork and inspiring words with even more people? Post your images on social media, and use the hashtag #coloringfaith. Also find more gorgeous coloring books at Coloringfaith.com.

To Get Started . . .

All you need is some colored pencils, felt-tip pens, watercolor paints, or even crayons—nothing fancy or expensive required. Even with just a few colors, you can create various depths of color and shade by layering colors and with varying pressures. Some sections of the coloring pages are embellished with metallic ink to add an extra glimmer to your completed pieces of art. You can't color over these areas, but they will complement your coloring choices, and they might even inspire you to try metallic pens! Perforated pages make it easy to remove each page for gifting or displaying in your own home.

The heavens declare the glory
of God; the skies proclaim
the work of his hands.

Psalm 19:1

Through him all things were
made; without him nothing was
made that has been made.

John 1:3

CAST ALL YOUR ANXIETY ON HIM
BECAUSE HE CARES FOR YOU.

1 Peter 5:7

Jesus asked, "What is the kingdom of God like? What shall I compare it to? It is like a mustard seed, which a man took and planted in his garden. It grew and became a tree, and the birds perched in its branches."

Luke 13:18–19

Lovely flowers are the smiles of God's goodness.

William Wilberforce

"I have loved you with an everlasting love."

Jeremiah 31:3

The waters are rising, but so am I.
I am not going under, but over.

Catherine Booth

"WHEN YOU PASS THROUGH THE WATERS, I WILL BE WITH YOU." ISAIAH 43:2

As the deer pants for streams of water,
so my soul pants for you, my God.

Psalm 42:1

You can do more than pray after you have prayed, but you cannot do more than pray until you have prayed.

A. J. Gordon

Pray continually.

1 Thessalonians 5:17

This is what the Lord says: "Stand at the crossroads and look; ask for the ancient paths, ask where the good way is, and walk in it, and you will find rest for your souls."

Jeremiah 6:16

In every situation, by prayer and petition,
with thanksgiving, present your requests to
God. And the peace of God, which transcends
all understanding, will guard your hearts
and your minds in Christ Jesus.

Philippians 4:6–7

As our Father makes many a flower to bloom unseen in the lonely desert, [let us] do all that we can do, as under God's eye, though no other eye ever take note of it.

Hudson Taylor

Keep me as the apple of your eye;
hide me in the shadow of your wings.

PSALM 17:8

Humble yourselves before the
Lord, and he will lift you up.

James 4:10

The early morning hour should
be dedicated to praise: do not
the birds set us the example?

Charles Spurgeon

I WILL SING OF YOUR STRENGTH, IN THE MORNING I WILL SING OF YOUR LOVE.

Psalm 59:16

The grass withers and the flowers fall, but
the word of our God endures forever.

Isaiah 40:8

How sweet are your words to my taste, sweeter than honey to my mouth!

Psalm 119:103

Thou hast created us for Thyself, and our
heart is not quiet until it rests in Thee.

Saint Augustine

"You will go out in joy and be led forth in peace; the mountains and hills will burst into song before you, and all the trees of the field will clap their hands."

Isaiah 55:12

A single sunbeam is enough to
drive away many shadows.

Saint Francis of Assisi

"I am the light of the world."

John 8:12

If God be our God, He will give us peace in trouble. When there is a storm without, He will make peace within. The world can create trouble in peace, but God can create peace in trouble.

Thomas Watson

"IN THIS WORLD YOU WILL HAVE TROUBLE. BUT TAKE HEART! I HAVE OVERCOME THE WORLD." JOHN 16:33

I will sing to the LORD all my life; I will sing praise to my God as long as I live.

Psalm 104:33

CHORDS THAT WERE BROKEN

WILL VIBRATE ONCE MORE.

Fanny Crosby

The LORD is near to all
who call on him.

Psalm 145:18

Help me, Lord, to remember that religion
is not to be confined to the church . . . nor
exercised only in prayer and meditation, but
that everywhere I am in Thy presence.

Susanna Wesley

The LORD their God will save his people on
that day as a shepherd saves his flock. They
will sparkle in his land like jewels in a crown.

Zechariah 9:16

"I AM THE GOOD SHEPHERD;
I KNOW MY SHEEP AND
MY SHEEP KNOW ME."

John 10:14

O for a thousand tongues to sing my great
Redeemer's praise, the glories of my God
and King, the triumphs of his grace!

Charles Wesley

The **Lord** has done great things for us,
and we are filled with joy.

Psalm 126:3

"I will make rivers flow on barren
heights, and springs within the valleys.
I will turn the desert into pools of water,
and the parched ground into springs."

Isaiah 41:18

We are the clay,
you are the potter.

Isaiah 64:8

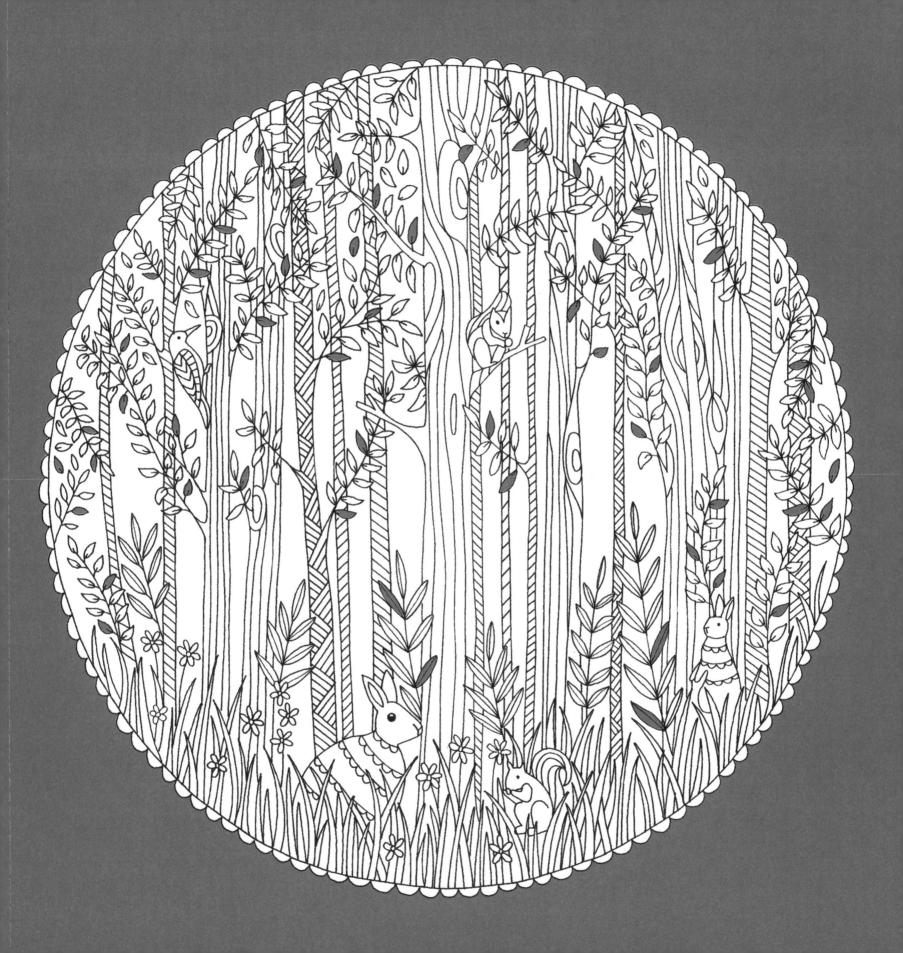

We have an advocate with the Father—
Jesus Christ, the Righteous One.

1 John 2:1

You alone are the LORD. You made the heavens, even the highest heavens, and all their starry host, the earth and all that is on it, the seas and all that is in them. You give life to everything, and the multitudes of heaven worship you.

Nehemiah 9:6

A perfect faith would lift us
absolutely above fear.

George MacDonald

Let the peace of
CHRIST
rule in your hearts.
COLOSSIANS 3:15

Sing to the Lᴏʀᴅ a new song; sing to the Lᴏʀᴅ, all the earth. Sing to the Lᴏʀᴅ, praise his name; proclaim his salvation day after day.

Psalm 96:1–2

Let everything that
has breath praise the LORD.

Psalm 150:6

The Lord is my shepherd, I lack nothing. He makes me lie down in green pastures, he leads me beside quiet waters, he refreshes my soul.

Psalm 23:1–3

"WHOEVER DRINKS THE WATER I GIVE THEM WILL NEVER THIRST."

John 4:14

Nature is God's greatest evangelist.

Jonathan Edwards

He is before all things, and in
him all things hold together.

Colossians 1:17

The LORD is good, a refuge in times of trouble. He cares for those who trust in him.

Nahum 1:7

I lift up my eyes to the mountains—
where does my help come from?
My help comes from the Lord, the
Maker of heaven and earth.

Psalm 121:1–2

GOD IS OUR REFUGE AND STRENGTH,
AN EVER-PRESENT HELP IN TROUBLE.

Psalm 46:1

Solitude with God repairs the
damage done by the fret and noise
and clamour of the world.

Oswald Chambers

"The LORD turn his face toward you and give you peace."

Numbers 6:26

The LORD gives wisdom; from his mouth
come knowledge and understanding.

Proverbs 2:6

"Come to me, all you who are weary and
burdened, and I will give you rest."

Matthew 11:28

"Look at the birds of the air; they do not sow or reap or store away in barns, and yet your heavenly Father feeds them. Are you not much more valuable than they?"

Matthew 6:26

Trust in the LORD
with all your heart.
Proverbs 3:5

"I am the vine; you are the branches.
If you remain in me and I in you,
you will bear much fruit."

John 15:5

"You will seek me and find me when
you seek me with all your heart."

Jeremiah 29:13

Heaven must receive him until the time comes for God
to restore everything, as he promised long ago.

Acts 3:21

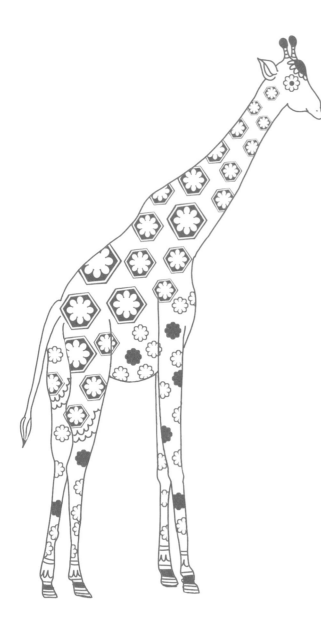

"I am making everything new!"

Revelation 21:5